THE TOP TEN HABITS OF MILLIONAIRES

THE
TOP 10
HABITS OF

MILLIONAIRES

TRANSFORM YOUR
THINKING – AND
GET RICH

KEITH CAMERON SMITH

PIATKUS

PIATKUS

First published in Great Britain in 2007 by Piatkus Books
First published in the US under the title of *The Top 10 Distinctions Between Millionaires and the Middle Class* in 2007 by Ballantine Books, an inprint of The Random House Publishing Group, a division of Random House, Inc., New York

A CIP catalogue record for this book
is available from the British Library

ISBN 978-0-7499-2857-5

Book design by Victoria Wong

Data manipulation by Phoenix Photosetting, Chatham, Kent
www.phoenixphotosetting.co.uk

Printed and bound in Great Britain by
Mackays Ltd, Chatham, Kent

Piatkus Books
An imprint of
Little, Brown Book Group
100 Victoria Embankment
London EC4Y 0DY

An Hachette Livre UK Company

www.piatkus.co.uk

Preface

Why I Wrote This Book

There are three reasons I wrote this book. The first is responsibility. I sincerely believe that each of us has a responsibility to share those things that produce good results in our own lives. Years ago I started seeking and finding very successful men and women who were generous enough with their time to teach me the attitudes, beliefs, and ideas that empowered them to live extraordinary lives. As I adopted their philosophies and made them a consistent part of my own life I also started to experience extraordinary results.

In addition to having some very powerful people teach me, I also read a lot of books to help develop my mind-set. This combination of personal mentors and reading has proven to be a significant part of the success journey for countless numbers of millionaires.

There are thousands of great books written on success, so why did I feel the need to write this one? The answer is because each book I read revealed a slightly different perspective on how to achieve success and fulfillment. And sometimes it is the smallest distinction that makes the biggest difference in our understanding. Sometimes someone can explain a certain principle in a certain way that makes a light go on in our minds. And so it is with this book. It reveals some different perspectives on success. Many of the ideas in this book have been taught for ages by many different teachers. There are several key points, however, that I have never read or heard anywhere. I learned them through my own experiences of success and failure, which I feel will resonate with many people.

I can honestly say that while writing this book I was in an inspired state. People are amazed when they ask me how long it took me to write this book and I tell them seven days. I sat down in a little cabin in the Smoky Mountains without any notes and just started typing. This book literally flowed out of the person I had become. Of course I have been studying success for years and learning from my own up-and-down adventures from being an entrepreneur. I don't just teach the habits in this book, I practice them every day. They are part of who I am.

The second reason I wrote this book is purpose. I believe we all have a song that we are destined to sing and this book is part of my song. I experience a strong sense of purpose every time I teach these principles and every time someone contacts me to share how they are producing positive results in their lives.

The third reason is legacy. These are some of the principles that I am teaching my own children to live by. One day when I am gone my children can pick this book up and remember some of the lessons their father taught them.

Some of the books I have read were written decades ago and some of them even centuries ago. Who knows where this book will be a hundred years from now? I believe these habits are timeless; they do not change. They will be just as useful a hundred years from now as they are today. So it is with a sense of responsibility, purpose, and legacy that I offer my understanding of these principles.

Contents

CONTENTS

A Note on the Order of the Habits

I have arranged the habit in descending order of importance. This arrangement is based on my own experiences as an entrepreneur as well as on the successes and failures of other millionaires. I believe that Habit 10 ("Millionaires think long-term.") is the necessary starting point for achieving success because it makes you focus on what you want. Most people focus on what they don't want and never set goals for what they do want. The importance of habits nine through two could be rearranged to fit your own life during the season that you are going through. For instance, habit number seven may be more important to you than habit number three at this time in your life. So whichever habit speaks to your heart the loudest, listen to it and learn what life is trying to teach you. As you work with these habits I think you will find that Habit 1 ("Millionaires ask themselves empowering questions.") is by far the most important to continually work with throughout your life. Always remember that success is a journey as well as a destination and the road is always under construction.

The Top
10
Distinctions Between
Millionaires
and the Middle Class

10

Millionaires think long-term.

Society can be broken down into five groups of people: the very poor, poor, middle class, rich, and very rich. Each group of people thinks differently about money. Very poor people think day to day. Poor people think week to week. Middle-class people think month to month. Rich people think year to year. And very rich people think decade to decade.

There are three primary goals that can be

found in the mind-sets of these five social groups. The primary goal for very poor and poor people is survival. The primary goal for middle-class people is comfort. And the primary goal for the rich and very rich is freedom.

The reason that very poor and poor people seek to survive and the middle class seeks to be comfortable is because they have a scarcity mentality. They believe there is not enough money for everyone to have more than enough. The rich and very rich know the truth: there is enough money for everyone to have more than enough.

What you believe about money has everything to do with how much money you will make. If you have a scarcity mentality, then you will seek to survive or just have enough to be comfortable. If you have an abundance mentality, you will seek freedom. The old saying "Seek and you will find" is true when it comes to your finances. You really do get what you look for in life. If you seek to survive, you will. If you seek to be comfortable, you will be. If you seek freedom, you will find it.

There is power in long-term thinking. It can and will make you rich if you make it a habit.

Let's look further at each of these groups of people.

Thinking day to day, as very poor people do, is where you will find day laborers and street beggars. They typically earn less than $10,000 a year.

Thinking week to week, as poor people do, is living paycheck to paycheck and barely making ends meet. Poor people typically earn $10,000 to $25,000 a year.

Thinking month to month, as middle-class people do, is being concerned with monthly bills, such as mortgage payments, car payments, credit card payments, and other revolving accounts. The middle class typically earns $25,000 to $100,000 a year.

Thinking year to year, as rich people do, is

where people start learning about fiscal responsibility, financial literacy, and investing. Rich people typically make $100,000 to $500,000 a year.

Thinking decade to decade, as the very rich do, is where you find business plans that reach far into the future. It is where people learn how to legally avoid taxes so they can keep their money working for them. It is where people learn how to pass their assets on to future generations without the government taking part of what they spent their lives building. Very rich people typically make well over $500,000 a year. Most very rich people consistently make a minimum of $1 million a year.

Stretch Your Thinking Further Into the Future

The longer you can stretch your thinking into the future, the richer you will become. Most multimillionaires I know personally have business plans that reach at least ten years into the future.

When I first started thinking year to year, my income really started to increase. I asked myself questions like: How can I double my income this year? How can I legally pay less in taxes this year? As I have seen this principle of long-term thinking in the lives of my mentors, it has challenged me to look further into my future. I now have business plans that go twenty years into the future. I spend time on a regular basis thinking about what I want my life to be like five, ten, and twenty years from now. Then I create plans for how to get there.

What would you like your life to be like ten years from now? Think about it and start planning for it. Thinking long-term requires patience. Patience is an asset in the life of millionaires. Impatience is a liability in the life of the middle class.

Middle-class people want instant gratification. I was like that for many years. Whatever I wanted, I charged to my credit card or put a

> Patience is an asset in the life of millionaires. Impatience is a liability in the life of the middle class.

little bit down and made payments on the balance. Now I wait for the things I want because my goal is more freedom, not comfort.

Rich and very rich people have developed the discipline of delayed gratification. Millionaires do today what others don't, so they can have tomorrow what others won't. The very poor, poor, and middle class will never be free. More and more freedom is the goal of the rich and very rich. They love to be in control of their lives.

The very poor, poor, and middle class have put control of their lives into the hands of others, which, ironically, are the hands of the rich and very rich.

Millionaires value freedom over comfort—and because they do, they get both.

Because the middle class values comfort over freedom, they will never be free.

Think Long-Term in Every Area of Life

I want you to be aware that this principle of thinking long-term not only applies to your financial life, but to every area of life. It is wise to think long-term in your relationships. When you do, you will show more respect to others and think from a win-win perspective.

If you think short-term in your relationships, you will be looking for what others can do for you and end up using people as a means to an end. If you are someone who always uses people for your own gain, then chances are you will be a lonely person, especially in your later years.

Millionaires develop long-term relationships, which also helps them with their long-term financial success. They think about how they can best serve their families, friends, and clients.

When you reach the end of your life, it is the relationships you have developed that make you truly rich. Ask yourself on a regular basis how

> When you reach the end of your life, it is the relationships you have developed that make you truly rich.

you can build deeper and stronger relationships with the people you love.

Just as there are people who are very poor financially, there are also people who are very poor emotionally. People who can't love or be patient or kind, people who can't forgive, and people who get angry easily are very poor emotionally. Focus on becoming rich emotionally as well as financially.

Becoming rich in your relationships is more than success. It is significance. It is fulfillment.

Financial success without relational fulfillment is not rewarding. Think long-term in your financial life and in your emotional life.

It is wise to think long-term about your physical health. If you do, then you will make the time to exercise your body and eat more healthily. If you don't think long-term in your health, then you will neglect exercise and eat too much junk. Chances are you will become overweight and live with a low amount of energy. Thinking long-term in your health empowers you with energy to become more successful financially.

Every area of life is connected, and thinking long-term in each area will improve every area.

> Every area of life is connected, and thinking long-term in each area will improve every area.

It is wise to think long-term in your mental life. What would you like to spend your life thinking about? Is there a certain subject that inspires you? What do you enjoy giving your mental energy to?

People who spend their lives thinking about things that excite and inspire them live with incredible peace of mind. People who could be considered very poor mentally are those who complain and spend their mental energy on things they dislike.

Mentally poor people live with a lot of stress. Would you like to increase your peace of mind? If so, then start thinking long-term in your mental life. Spend your mental energy on the subjects you enjoy. Dedicate your life to the fields of interests that inspire you. Find a way to make money in the areas you enjoy thinking about.

This is a secret of many millionaires: they do what they love to do to make money. This makes them rich mentally and financially. Think long-term in every area of your life, not just financially.

> This is a secret of many millionaires: they do what they love to do to make money.

Set More Long-Term Goals

In order to move from the poor to the middle class, or from the middle class to the rich, or from the rich to the very rich, just start planning your life further into the future. Set more long-term goals for your life. People overestimate what they can accomplish in one year and underestimate what they can accomplish in ten.

When you have long-term goals you will find it easier to develop perseverance. All millionaires have had to persevere through challenges in their lives. In order to see your dreams fulfilled you have to become a "whatever it takes" kind of person. Middle-class people give up when the pressure is on. Since they value comfort, they don't persevere when the going gets tough. Millionaires go the second mile, and the third, and the fourth. They do whatever it takes to experience abundance. Since they think long-term, they keep on keeping on until they achieve abundance and freedom.

Millionaires think long-term.

9

Millionaires talk about ideas.

If I spend a few minutes listening to you talk, I can tell you where you are headed in life. Your words reveal your heart and mind. They give an accurate picture of your future.

What do you spend your time talking about? Your words are like a ship's rudder. They determine which direction you are going in life. Millionaires spend most of their time talking about ideas and very little time talking about things or other people. The middle class rarely talks about ideas and spends the majority of its time talking about things and other people.

Big, Average, Small

I once saw a plaque in a businessman's office that said, "Big people talk about ideas, average people talk about things, and small people talk about other people." That is worth repeating. "Big people talk about ideas, average people talk about things, and small people talk about other people."

What do you spend your time talking about? Ideas, things, or people?

I am sure you have heard the old saying "There are three types of people, those who make things happen, those who watch things happen, and those who say what happened."

A deeper look into these two statements reveals a secret of the very successful. Many millionaires are creative. They spend time thinking

> "There are three types of people, those who make things happen, those who watch things happen, and those who say what happened."

about new ideas. When working on projects, they go into an option-thinking mode and look for several possibilities.

To become more successful you must continually expand your mind. In a world where everything is changing fast, you would be wise to spend time thinking of new ways of doing things.

Millionaires talk about ideas and make things happen. The middle class talks about things and watches things happen. The very poor talk about other people and ask, "What happened?"

Talking About Things

Middle-class people talk about things that came from a millionaire's idea. They talk about things like cars, sports, entertainment, music, and vacations.

Millionaires own the car companies. Millionaires own the sports teams. Millionaires produce the movies and television shows. Millionaires produce the music. Millionaires own the vacation spots. The middle class spends its money on the things that were created by a millionaire's idea.

Let's look more closely at entertainment. The middle class and the very poor are often Hollywood's biggest fans. They live for the gossip. They can't wait to see who did what. They are glued to their television sets.

Entertainment has its place, but it must be kept in balance. Sure, millionaires enjoy entertainment, but they don't spend much time talking about it. One of the reasons the middle class and the very poor love entertainment so much is because they are easily impressed with fame and fortune. Millionaires choose fortune over fame. They are not easily impressed with the superficial lifestyles of so-called stars.

People who are easily impressed with others are often insecure and confused about what they want in life. Millionaires are secure in who they are and what they want. When you are clear on who you are and what you want in life, you will become secure and successful.

Talking About People

Oftentimes the middle class and the very poor are poor financially because they are poor emotionally. You can't become rich without building good relationships. If you spend much time talking negatively about others, it will cost you emotionally and financially. Talking about people behind their backs is immature ignorance.

Millionaires respect people. They give people the benefit of the doubt and realize that people are doing the best they know how to do.

We can always find something someone is doing that we don't like or approve of. I suggest you look for what people are doing right and compliment them on it.

Millionaires are complimentary people. They understand the wisdom of making people feel important. Tearing down people is foolish because it puts you into a negative attitude and often traps you there. Don't get caught in the trap of talking about other people. It affects you in a negative way, more than you may realize.

Stop criticizing and start complimenting. You will feel better, and doors of opportunity will start to open.

People love to be praised. Learn to praise people and you will find that people will do whatever they can to help you.

Millionaires do talk about things and people, but not in the same way that the middle class does. Millionaires talk about the great idea someone had. They talk about people who create wealth with their ideas and discuss what they can learn from them.

One of my multimillionaire friends and I swap notes from the different seminars we attend. Anytime we learn something new about one of our business interests, we share it with each other. When we talk about other people, we discuss the ideas we learned from them, how they implement those ideas in their businesses, and how those ideas seem to be working for them.

When millionaires talk about things and other people, it always seems to boil down to ideas.

Talking About Ideas

Why do millionaires spend their time talking about ideas? The answer is because they understand that it takes ideas to make money. The middle class thinks that you must have money to make money. Millionaires know better. They understand that the right idea will attract the money they need.

Ideas are the most valuable asset in the world. People who come up with great ideas end up with great wealth. Everything you see first started as an idea in someone's mind. If you

> Ideas are the most valuable asset in the world.

want to become richer, then spend your time thinking about new ideas. When you get an idea, discuss it with people who are successful.

Major point here! Do not discuss your ideas with people who are unsuccessful. If you do, they will discourage you. Millionaires talk about ideas with other millionaires. They don't discuss their ideas with people who have a limited mentality. The middle-class mentality is limited

> Money is powerful, but ideas are even more powerful.

because it doesn't acknowledge the power of ideas. Money is powerful, but ideas are even more powerful.

What You Can Do

Taking time to dream every day increases your creativity. When you consciously use your imagination on a regular basis, then you will start a constant flow of ideas that can make you money. Millionaires do not have a problem finding something to do to make money. If anything, they have a problem choosing which ideas they are going to act on.

Here are a couple of simple ways to talk about ideas more than things and other people:

1. Change your vocabulary.

Talking about ideas requires a different vocabulary than the middle class uses. Use words like *possible* instead of *impossible, can* instead of *can't,* and *I will* instead of *I should.*

Millionaires have positive vocabularies. This is not "be positive" hocus-pocus. Words are powerful. Listen to your middle-class friends and you will find their conversations are much more pessimistic than optimistic. Millionaires speak with a strong faith. They believe they can turn their ideas into reality—and they do.

2. Stop complaining and start learning.

When the middle class complains, it is talking about things and other people. I believe that whatever you complain about, you get more of. Complain about bills or debts and you get more of them. Complain about people treating you unfairly and you will continue to be treated unfairly. Complain about how bad your job is and it will get worse. The power of your words creates the experiences of your life.

> The power of your words creates the experiences of your life.

Millionaires are not whiners. I can't recall a

single time when I heard one of my multimillion-aire mentors complain about anything.

The words you use reveal your heart and mind. Is your heart full of disrespect for the people in your life? Is your mind full of negative thoughts? Listen to the words you speak and you will know. People who complain are literally cursing themselves.

If you want to stop cursing yourself and start blessing yourself, then stop complaining and start being thankful. Gratitude is one of the greatest powers in the universe. Focusing on what you are thankful for brings more of it into your life. Talk

> The next time you are tempted to complain, ask yourself, "What is life trying to teach me?"

about ideas, things, and people you appreciate and your life will be transformed.

The next time you are tempted to complain, ask yourself, "What is life trying to teach me?"

There is always a lesson to be learned when something doesn't go your way or when things appear to be difficult. The lessons of life come to teach us to look at life from new perspectives. This leads to new ideas.

Learn to see from different points of views and you will have exciting new ideas to talk about.

Millionaires talk about ideas.

8

Millionaires embrace change.

Change can be positive or negative. The problem is, we don't know which it will be when change first presents itself. People don't mind positive change. They actually want positive change. The problem with the middle class is it assumes change will be negative most of the time. Millionaires assume that all change, positive or negative, will benefit them.

Nido Qubein says, "For the timid in our

society, change is frightening. For the comfortable, change is threatening. But for the truly confident among us, change is opportunity."

Learn to Embrace Change

How well do you handle change, especially unexpected change? Learning to deal well with change is a must if you are to become a millionaire. Millionaires embrace change because they know it always brings an opportunity for growth.

> Millionaires embrace change because they know it always brings an opportunity for growth.

People who are insecure resist change. People who are confident welcome it. Millionaires are confident. Confidence is acquired through preparation and hard work. Confidence is the result of working on yourself. It is the benefit of proving yourself to yourself. It is knowing you can handle whatever comes your way. Confidence is believing you can do whatever you choose to.

Choice versus Wish

Millionaires choose to be rich. The middle class wishes it were rich. There's a big difference between a choice and a wish. A choice is backed by a belief that you can do it. A wish is backed by a doubt that you can.

Doubt is a code word for fear. The middle class is afraid it can't or won't become rich.

What's inside of you, a belief you can do it or a fear that you can't? Change shows you what you're made of. It reveals what's inside of you. If you get angry when change comes, it's because you have anger inside of you. If you get worried when change occurs, it's because you are fearful. If you complain when change happens, it is because you are ungrateful. Millionaires don't complain or worry or get angry when change occurs. They look for the opportunity it brings. Change always gives you the opportunity to grow and become stronger.

See the Opportunity in Change

People in the middle class fear change because they don't know if they are strong enough to handle it. The number one reason people resist change is fear.

Fear blinds you to opportunities. When you develop confidence and learn to accept change, you will be able to see the opportunity it is bringing to you.

> Fear blinds you to opportunities.

Someone once said, "In times of change, the learners will inherit the earth, while the learned will find themselves well equipped to deal with a world that no longer exists." Change teaches us new things that we need to learn. The more we learn, the stronger and more confident we become.

> Change teaches us new things that we need to learn.

Confidence is strength. The more confident

you become, the more prepared you are to take advantage of opportunities when they appear. You never know when an opportunity may present itself.

The middle class thinks millionaires got lucky and were in the right place at the right time. It's not enough to be in the right place at the right time. You have to be the right person, in the right place, at the right time; otherwise you won't even see the opportunity. Learning to embrace change assures that you are becoming a person who can profit from life's opportunities.

The future belongs to those who can change with the times. The purpose of change is to change us. Learning to accept change is the first step to being more confident. Allowing change to change you is the real purpose of it. People are born to learn and grow. Change is life's way of making sure we do that.

Learn to Fly

Resisting change is like an eaglet not wanting to leave the warmth and comfort of his nest. Eventually, momma eagle starts changing the warm and comfortable environment by removing her nice, soft down feathers from the nest. Before you know it, sharp sticks and twigs are poking the eaglet. "Why are you doing this to me, Momma?" he screams.

Momma eagle says, "Because it's time you learn how to fly."

Change is life's way of teaching you how to fly. The next time you ask, "Why is this happening to me?" remember momma eagle's answer to her baby.

Sometimes we don't know what we can do until we have to. Ask someone to think back to a difficult time of his life, when life threw him a curveball. He will probably say, "It was the best thing that ever happened to me."

Almost everyone has an experience like that. Let's learn a lesson from ourselves and realize that change is always meant for our good.

Change is good! The quicker you accept change when it comes, the sooner you will learn the lesson. The quicker you learn the lesson, the sooner you will start enjoying your new strength.

It feels great when you increase your confidence. Enjoy the feeling of growing and getting stronger. Embrace change when it comes and learn how to fly.

Millionaires embrace change.

7

Millionaires take calculated risks.

The middle class is trapped in the rat race because it doesn't take risks. The only way out of the rat race is to take risks. The only way out of the rat race is to take risks. No, that is not a typo. I intentionally wrote it twice. In fact, let me write it one more time. The only way out of the rat race is to take risks. If you take risk out of life, you take opportunity out of life.

Taking a risk doesn't mean taking a shot in the

> If you take risk out of life, you take opportunity out of life.

dark. Millionaires take CALCULATED risks. What does *calculated* mean? It means to gain knowledge first and to consider the consequences of failing before taking action.

Use Knowledge to Overcome Fear

Millionaires are not afraid to take risks. That's not to say they don't have fears to deal with. Both millionaires and the middle class have fears. The way you handle fear, however, determines the results you will get in life.

Millionaires overcome fear and the middle class submits to it.

Millionaires overcome fear with knowledge. Fear is darkness and knowledge is light. Light causes darkness to disappear; knowledge causes fear to disappear.

Millionaires educate themselves before taking risks, and then they consider the consequences of failing. Millionaires don't throw their money around and hope for a return.

Millionaires practice risk management. One of the simplest ways to manage risk I learned from my mentor Nido Qubein. He taught me to ask these three questions:

1. What's the best thing that could happen?
2. What's the worst thing that could happen?
3. What's the most likely thing to happen?

If you can live with the worst thing that could happen and if the most likely thing to happen will get you closer to your goals, then go for it! If you aren't able to handle the worst that could happen and if the most likely thing to happen doesn't get you closer to your goals, then don't do it. The next time you have an opportunity to take a risk, ask yourself these three questions. They have given me the insight I needed to make wise decisions.

I see three primary fears in the middle class that stop people from taking the actions that create success. They are the fear of failure, the fear of rejection, and the fear of loss.

The Fear of Failure

It is not a matter of *if* you will fail, it is a matter of *when*. Millionaires understand that failure is part of the path to success. They do not fear failure; they embrace it when it comes and become wiser. The reason the middle class fears failure is because it thinks failure is bad. Millionaires think failure is good. It gives them the opportunity to learn and grow.

If you fear failure, you will not take risks. Any time you take a risk there is the possibility of failing. If you learn to see failure as a positive, then you will be able to take more risks. Your perception of and response to failure will determine the level of success you can achieve.

Failure is one of life's many teachers. Failure is

life's way of correcting us. When millionaires fail, they learn and try again. When middle-class people fail, they stop taking risks. A common phrase for the middle class is: I tried that before and I'm not doing it again.

> Failure is one of life's many teachers.

The middle class gives up after failing while millionaires keep going. You must keep going after you fail in order to achieve success.

The Fear of Rejection

The middle class puts too much importance on the acceptance of others. We all want others to accept us. We also want to be successful. Here's a key to success: you must want to succeed more than you want the acceptance of other people.

> You must want to succeed more than you want the acceptance of other people.

Millionaires desire success more than they desire acceptance. In order to be successful you will have to take risks and, if you fail, some people may reject you. The funny thing is, if you succeed, some people will still reject you!

Someone once said one third of people will like you, one third won't, and one third doesn't care either way. Millionaires understand they can't please everybody. If you are addicted to the approval of people, this will keep you from taking risks. You must not let your need for acceptance keep you from taking risks. Simply understand that some people are going to reject you no matter what you do, and then do what you need to do to succeed.

The Fear of Loss

Millionaires play to win. The middle class plays not to lose. Huge difference! Can you imagine if a football team played defense the entire game? Their chance of winning would be zero. If you fear loss, you will only play defense when it comes to your money and your chance of financial freedom will be zero.

People who play not to lose are always saying they should have done this or that. The biggest gap in the world is between *I should* and *I did*.

> The biggest gap in the world is between *I should* and *I did*.

Millionaires can say, "I did." The middle class is always saying, "I should." When you take risks, you may lose some money; accept it and go on. Just as failure is part of success, losing is part of winning.

Did you know most millionaires have lost money several times in their lives? Some millionaires have been through bankruptcy more than once before winning the money game. If you want to win, you must overcome the fear of loss. The fear of loss keeps the middle class sitting on the sidelines of life. If you want to win, you must play to win. Playing not to lose will cause you to lose.

Live Like You Were Dying

When I speak at live events I will often include a section about living like you were dying. In that section I discuss a survey done among a group of elderly people over the age of ninety. They were asked, "If you had life to live over again, what would you do differently?"

There were three answers that kept coming up repeatedly. Would you care to guess one of them? One was that they would take more risks! Did you get that? When you are at the end of your life, you will have more regrets over the things you didn't do than the things you did. Taking risks assures that you won't have to live with the pain of regret. Don't get to the end of your life and say, "I wish I had." Overcome your fears with faith and take some risks.

> When you are at the end of your life, you will have more regrets over the things you didn't do than the things you did.

Let me give you the other two answers. They said they would take more time to reflect on the good moments of their lives and appreciate them, and on the bad times to learn from them. The third most common answer was they would do more things that would live on after they were gone. Now, if you're going to do something that will live on after you're gone, you're going to have to take some risks. People who are re-membered took risks.

Our elders have spoken: take more risks, re-flect more, and do more things that will live on after you are gone. If you can't learn from a group of people over the age of ninety, then you just can't learn. I repeat, if you take the risk out of life, you take the opportunity out of life.

Remember, knowledge is light and fear is darkness. Shine the light into the darkness and you will have the courage to take action. Millionaires overcome

> **Knowledge is light and fear is darkness.**

their fears and take action. The middle class submits to its fears and lives with regrets. Be able to say *I did* instead of *I should*. Calculate your risks by educating yourself and asking those three questions.

Millionaires take calculated risks.

6

Millionaires continually learn and grow.

Why is it that million-dollar homes have libraries? Is it just a coincidence that million-dollar homes have them and $100,000 homes don't? I don't think so.

Most millionaires I know read one book a week. In my circle of influence, we are always recommending books and audio programs to each other. One of my friends has spent $500,000 studying success. I have spent $100,000 on my success education. If you have a middle-class mentality you are probably thinking, I don't have that kind of money to spend to learn how to make money.

I didn't say that my friends or I spent all that money at one time. We continue to invest in our knowledge as we make more money. Success is a process. If a percentage of your income isn't going toward a finan-cial education, you will

Success is a process.

stay trapped in the middle class. The more money you spend on financial knowledge, the more money you will make.

The Power of Books and Coaches

You can start with books. I promise you, mil-lionaires read and read and read. Books are so inexpensive compared to how much the knowl-edge they contain is worth. Are you aware that you can learn a concept in only a few hours from a book that took someone years to develop?

More people than ever are becoming millionaires because they are compressing time and
learning financial secrets that took others years
to discover. I feel like some of the $20 books I
have read were worth $20,000 because of what
I learned from them.

In addition to books and audio programs,
millionaires also pay for advice from people who
have specialized knowledge in a field they need
to learn about. The middle class looks for free
advice. Free advice can often be the most expen-
sive advice. Oftentimes, free advice ends up cost-
ing you something. Free advice is usually just the
opinion of someone who thinks he knows what
he is talking about but doesn't have any real-
world experience.

Millionaires don't put much value on free advice. Millionaires learn from people who have
been there, done it, and are preferably still doing
it. This is where your financial education expense will start adding up.

The books in my success library are probably valued at about $20,000. The investment I have made for personal coaching and mentoring is five times that amount. Notice I didn't say, "The price I paid," I said, "The investment I have made."

It's difficult to put a value on the knowledge you gain from someone who has real-world experience. A good coach or mentor charges a price, but millionaires see this expense as an investment. I believe everyone should have a coach. Why not? Every great athlete you can think of has one. Why shouldn't you have one if you want to build great wealth?

Invest in Your Financial Education

A weekend-long wealth-building event I attended cost $12,500. One of the millionaires there said he gained one piece of knowledge that would be worth an additional $10 million when he applied it to his current business. Is it worth $12,500 to gain the knowledge that could increase your income by $10 million? Of course it is.

I realize the middle class can't start out by going to events that require this size investment. But they can read a $20 book that could be worth $20,000 to them if they apply the knowledge they gain.

Millionaires invest in their knowledge with people who have achieved the successes that they want for themselves. When I first started investing in real estate I bought a $25 audiobook that gave me the knowledge and courage to get started. Next I bought one of those real estate programs from an infomercial that cost $200. With the knowledge I gained and applied from it, I made almost $100,000 the next year. After that, I invested in a one-year program that cost $4,000 and made over $200,000 the next year.

(I am leaving out the details, because I am only making the point that the more you invest in your knowledge, the more you will make when you apply it.) Wisdom is the application of knowledge.

Most middle-class people stay at the same level of income year after year because their knowledge stays at the same level year after year. One reason for this is because they think learning ended with school. Millionaires are students of life. They continually learn from the circumstances of their lives.

> Millionaires are students of life.

A common question millionaires ask is: "What can I learn from this?" In contrast, the middle class asks: "Why does this always happen to me?" Because it doesn't learn the lessons life is trying to teach, the middle class is destined to go through the situation again.

I like what a preacher said about this. He

said, "You never fail one of God's tests. You just keep taking them until you pass."

How true! The question, "Why does this always happen to me?" implies it is happening *again*. The only reason the same bad situation arises again and again is because your knowledge remains the same. You must continually learn and grow to become and stay a millionaire. If you become a millionaire and stop your learning process, then chances are you won't remain a millionaire for long.

Knowledge Is a Seed

Millionaires focus on personal growth. They believe that to have more, they must become more. They see growing as one of the main purposes of life. Growth takes time. Be patient with yourself as you gain knowledge. Realize that knowledge is a seed and it takes time for seeds to grow into trees that bear fruit. Every time you read a book, you are either planting another seed or watering some that are already in your mind.

Millionaires read books about money and how to build better relationships. They read about the power of the mind. They read about the successes and failures of others.

Millionaires are serious students of a successful life, not just financial success. They continually look for new ways of thinking and acting that can produce more fulfillment in their lives.

Study What You Love

The secret to being a lifelong learner is to study what you love. One of the biggest differences I have seen between millionaires and the middle class is that millionaires focus on what they

> The secret to being a lifelong learner is to study what you love.

enjoy doing. They continually learn more about the subjects that inspire them. The reason millionaires study about every area of life is because they love life.

The middle class thinks millionaires love money too much. In my experience, that is simply not true. What is true is that millionaires love what they can do for their families and others with their abundance.

Millionaires who are greedy and afraid of losing their money are not truly successful. True success involves peace and contentment.

Study success and learn how to make money, but also learn how to be content with where you are while in pursuit of what you want.

I repeat, millionaires love life. They love what they do to make money and they love having money—but they don't love money above life itself. If you love money more than your family or yourself, you have been deceived by it and will never achieve true success.

Know Your Priorities

I know people in the high end of the middle class who are constantly striving for more. They love money too much and will continue to be unsatisfied with their results until they learn to be content with who they are rather than what they have.

I believe many millionaires achieved their success because they had their priorities in the right order. I mention this in my discussion about learning and growing because some people do get out of balance when they start pursuing financial wealth. They give money too much attention and neglect their families and/or their health. Don't be one of those people who lose their families and/or their health while pursuing financial prosperity. Money is important, but it is not worth losing the things that matter most.

Please study financial success and personal fulfillment. It feels good to have money, it feels

even better to have deep and meaningful relationships with those you love, and it feels great
to have both. Learn to love yourself and others,
and learn to earn massive amounts of money.

Millionaires continually learn and grow.

5

Millionaires work for profits.

People who work for wages end up earning enough to live on but not much more. It is rare for someone to make enough money from an hourly or salary position to become financially free. Millionaires understand this and choose to work for profits instead of wages. Wages are the pay you receive for the work you do. Profits are the result of buying something for one price and selling it for a higher price. Millionaires are in the sales business.

If you depend on wages for your income, then your income will always be extremely limited. If you learn to earn profits, then the sky is the limit.

> If you learn to earn profits, then the sky is the limit.

It has been said that over 90 percent of people who make more than $100,000 a year are in some form of sales. I believe this is true. All of my multimillionaire friends and mentors work for profits. Not one of them works for wages.

Here is a short summary of my personal experiences with profits and wages:

When I was in elementary school I sold cinnamon-flavored toothpicks to the other kids. I would buy a bottle of cinnamon oil from a

local pharmacy, soak toothpicks in it each even-
ing, take them to school the next day, and come
home with cash. The bottle of cinnamon oil cost
less than $10. It took me a couple weeks to use
it up and sell all the toothpicks. I can remember
making about $20 profit in about two weeks.
Not bad for an elementary school kid.

In middle school, my parents would give me
$3 a day for lunch. On the way to school I
would buy thirty large sticks of gum from a con-
venience store for ten cents a piece and sell them
for twenty-five cents each when I got to school.
Do the math. I turned $3 into $7.50 before
lunch each day, then used $1 to buy a milk shake
for lunch, and would come home with $6.50.

Somehow, when I was in high school, the
conditioning of society got to me and I went
looking for a job—because that's what everyone
said I should do. For nearly ten years I worked
for wages and was never satisfied with the
money I made. It always bothered me when I

saw the amount of taxes taken out of each pay-check. During those ten years I did buy and sell a few other things to make extra money once in a while.

For instance, after high school I took up golf. I can remember going to golf courses with a friend and wading in the shallow ponds for golf balls. We'd find a few hundred balls in only a couple of hours. I would sell them the next day to a used golf club shop. My friend and I would make $40 to $50 each for just two hours of work! That was big money for me, because my jobs only paid $5 an hour.

Nowadays you can buy golf balls at Wal-Mart that have been retrieved from ponds. I was on to a million-dollar idea way back then, but didn't know it! I made thousands of dollars over the next couple of years selling lost golf balls. Meanwhile I kept working for wages because my middle-class mentality told me that was what I was supposed to do.

My family was in the low end of the middle class. My dad sold auto parts to small garages around town and rarely made more than $25,000 a year. I expressed to him how unhappy I was with making such a small amount of money. He suggested I start an auto parts route in a nearby town. He said I could make more than my job now paid, with less work. I never liked the auto parts business, so I didn't take his advice.

I kept working odd jobs until I found one working at a golf course as a cart attendant. It was the perfect job! I earned $5 an hour plus a few tips, and I could look for golf balls while waiting for the carts to be returned in the evenings. I was averaging $8 an hour plus the golf ball money. I did this for a couple years and during that time my golf game greatly improved. I was shooting in the 70s and decided to become a golf pro. (This was when the Ladies Professional Golf Association was just about to open their headquarters in Daytona Beach.)

I applied for the apprentice position working in the pro shop and got it. My wage was now $8 an hour, but I didn't get tips or have time to look for golf balls, so my income remained the same. I didn't care though, because I was going to be a pro and make big bucks, or so I thought.

I took the PGA test for my pro card a couple of times but never broke 80. My nerves couldn't handle it. So I set my sights on being a club pro. I sat down with the club pro at the LPGA course where I worked and asked him how long before I would start making good money. He busted my bubble when he said, "Keith, I am going to be honest with you. You are going to have to pay your dues. It will take at least five or six years before you can move up."

I felt sick when I heard that. I was not willing to wait five or six years before making more money. Once again, I went whining to my dad. This time he suggested something I decided to try. He recommended I sell R-12 Freon for car air conditioners. This was when the government was taxing R-12 Freon heavily and the prices were going up like crazy. He said I could buy kegs of Freon for $180 and sell them for $200 or $210. Dad was right. I bought a few kegs to try it and sold them right away. A few weeks later the price for Freon in all retail stores went to $250 a keg yet my wholesale price only increased to $200.

I would sell a couple of kegs, make $100 in a few hours, and then take the rest of the day off to go to the beach. I had one customer who would buy ten kegs at a time, so every few weeks, when he'd order, I'd make $500 in a day and take the rest of the week off to play and have fun! Boy, was I stupid! I was stupid for two reasons. One, because I could have made a lot more money back then, and two, I thought it was going to last. It didn't. After a few months, the price of Freon had escalated to $500 a keg.

The only people who had it were the big companies that had stocked up on it. And they weren't wholesaling any.

As fate would have it, I went to an auction one night, just for fun. I saw things being sold for what seemed to be incredibly low prices, especially furniture. I started buying items at auctions and taking them to the flea market and reselling them. Going to the auction each week, I came to know a man who owned a used-furniture store. He drove nice trucks, owned a boat, and lived in a big house on several acres of land. I thought he was rich (because I was so poor), although in reality he was just at the higher end of the middle class.

Seeing his success, I realized I needed to open my own used-furniture store—and that's exactly what I did. Up until that point, my income had never been more than $20,000 a year. Immediately my income almost tripled. I earned over

$50,000 the first year I owned the furniture store. A year after opening the store, I got married.

Driving around one day, I noticed a going-out-of-business sign in the window of a small furniture store. I stopped to inquire if the location was going to be available because it was a much nicer place than where my store currently was.

I learned the building would be available the following month. The man who owned it was next door and could tell me about the lease. So I walked over and met the man. I was pleasantly surprised to find out that the rent was only $100 more per month than I was now paying.

I called my wife and told her we were moving our business. Originally we were going to open the same type of store, selling higher-end used furniture, but in the course of talking to the owners who were moving out, we found out that their business was more successful than ours, so we decided to copy what they had been doing, which was selling brand-new bedroom sets, daybeds, and futons. Our income went up to about $70,000 the first year we were there.

During the course of owning that little store, I met the man whom I bought futon frames from. He owned two futon stores and seemed to be doing very well with them. The first time my wife saw his stores, she thought we should stop selling bedroom sets and daybeds and only sell futons, like he was.

I resisted at first, but after a month or so I decided to give it a try because we were already selling ten futons for every one bedroom set and daybed. Guess what? We had found a niche in the industry and our income went up again! We were earning about $100,000 a year.

I have left out several details and the story keeps going, but I'll end it now by saying we started investing in real estate. We bought seven properties within a couple of years and reached a net worth of over $1 million. Had I continued working for

KEITH CAMERON SMITH

wages at the golf course, I might have been making $12 an hour, which is barely $20,000 a year
after the taxes are taken out.

You see, when you work for wages, they can
only increase gradually. When you work for
profits, you have the potential of increasing your
income dramatically in a short time. I haven't
worked for wages in almost ten years now and I
never plan on working for wages again. If you
want to become a millionaire, you must learn to
work for profits.

Millionaires work for profits.

4

Millionaires believe they must be generous.

One day I was in a sub shop buying myself lunch. A man about nineteen years old served me. The total came to just under $5. I paid him with a $10 bill. When he handed me a $5 bill and some change, I put the coins in my pocket and handed him the $5 bill. "Here, this is for you," I said.

For a second, he looked confused, then he said, "Are you serious?"

"Yes," I said.

"Holy crap!" he exclaimed. He couldn't believe it.

His response to my giving him only $5 was amazing.

About a week later I returned to the same sub shop. This time an older black woman served me. My bill was almost $8, so I paid her with a $20 bill. When she gave me the change, I kept a couple of dollars and gave her a $10 bill. "Here, this is for you," I said.

She said, "For real?"

"Yes," I said. "God bless you."

She then emphatically said, "Hallelujah! Thank you, Jesus!"

Her response made me smile as I walked out the front door. I couldn't have bought anything for $5 or $10 that gave me the pleasure I enjoyed from their reactions.

Learn to Be Generous

Being generous is fun. It feels great when you give from the heart. I have given total strangers money on numerous occasions, and will continue to do so throughout my life.

> It feels great when you give from the heart.

It's a good habit to be generous; to make sure money never controls you.

I once heard a spiritual teacher tell of a test you can do to see if you possess your money or if it possesses you. The test: give it away. If you can do that, then you possess your money. If you can't, then your money possesses you.

More Stories

One time I was driving down one of the main streets in town. It was about 9:00 P.M. It was rainy and there was a chill in the air. I passed a young woman walking on the side of the road. I am not in the habit of picking up strange women but I felt bad for her having to walk in the cold rain. I turned my truck around and went back to ask if she needed a ride. She accepted and got in the front seat beside me. I asked her where she was headed and she told me.

It was quiet for a few seconds. Then she asked, "Can I touch you?" I had picked up a prostitute!

I laughed and said, "No, you can't touch me."

With a frightened voice she said, "You're a cop, aren't you?"

I laughed again and said, "No, I am not a cop."

"Then why won't you let me touch you?"

I showed her my wedding ring and said, "Because I am a very happily married man."

She sincerely apologized. I asked her, "Look, if I give you some money, will you not go out on the streets tonight?"

She immediately replied, "Yes! Definitely!"

I asked her what made her feel like she had to

resort to prostitution to make money. The tone of her voice dropped when she answered. "I have two small children at home and I have to get groceries for them. My mom is watching them for me right now." I sensed she was telling me the truth so I offered to take her to the grocery store to buy whatever they needed. She hesitantly accepted.

When we were in the grocery store she seemed reluctant to put anything in the cart. She chose a couple of items, like milk and bread. I asked, "What else do you need?" She didn't know what to say, so I suggested, "What about some peanut butter and jelly or cereal?" She agreed. I also picked up some cookies and a few other items. The total was a bit over $40.

She thanked me several times when we were in the parking lot. We got back in my truck and I asked her where she lived. She lived in a trailer park about three miles from where I had picked her up. When we pulled up to the trailer, I noticed a lady standing in the doorway.

The young woman jumped out of my truck and shouted, "Mom! Mom! I met this guy and he went and bought us groceries. Now the kids can have milk in the morning!" Then she said, "And he loves his wife, let me tell you!"

Her mother stepped a little further out of the doorway and asked me, "Are you an angel?"

"Well, maybe," I replied.

The young woman handed the bags of groceries to her mom to take inside and said thank you several more times. She was about to step inside herself when I said, "Wait a minute. Come here. I have something else for you." She came over to me and I gave her $100. She didn't know what to say. I said, "Here's some money for groceries, for later in the week. Have a good night." She thanked me yet again. I got back in my truck and headed home.

There are so many opportunities for us to be generous every day. Being generous is a sure way to be happy. Being greedy is a sure way to be miserable.

I know I didn't solve that young woman's problems for the long term, but who knows what might have happened to her that night? One reason I write books and teach seminars on success is to give people the knowledge they can use to make a long-term improvement, if they choose.

Although I have many other stories about generosity, I will share just two more with you here.

One day I was sitting in my truck at a park next to the Halifax River. My dad was with me and we were discussing a business idea I had about another furniture store. While we were talking about different possibilities, I noticed a young black man sitting in an old beat-up car next to us. He was staring off into space and appeared to be in deep thought. I felt an urge to give him $100. When my dad and I were done talking, I got out of my truck and walked over to his car.

His window was down and I said, "Excuse me." He was startled and looked up at me. Before he could say anything I said, "I just want to give this to you and say God bless you." He looked at the $100 bill, slowly took it, but didn't say a word. He was speechless. I felt awkward and said, "Well, God bless you."

As I took a step away from his car, he said, "Wait a minute." I stepped back up to his window and he said, "I was just sitting here reading this book." I hadn't noticed the book in his hands. He turned it over so I could see the title. It was a small book titled *The Creative Power of God*.

I smiled and once again said, "Well, God

bless you." He didn't say anything in response so I got back in my truck and left.

Once again, I know I didn't solve his problems for the long term, but who knows what he was thinking about? Maybe he had prayed for something and the $100 was a sign for him. The point of the story is: be generous.

Not all millionaires are generous, but the happy ones are! Most millionaires believe in the law of sowing and reaping. They see money as a seed. Millionaires know that if they are generous, they will receive more in return.

> Not all millionaires are generous, but the happy ones are!

Millionaires are not only good givers; they are also good receivers. They have a very different belief about receiving than the middle class does. They believe they deserve to receive because they are generous. In my experience, people in the middle class have a hard time receiving. I believe it is because they don't feel they deserve it. How can they, if they are not generous?

One more story . . .

My wife and I were at a conference in Charlotte, North Carolina. It was about 11:30 P.M., our meeting had ended, and we were hungry. We drove around and found a Domino's Pizza parlor in a small strip mall. I went in to order our pizza and came back out into the parking lot to wait for it. I was standing next to our car, my wife was in the car with the door open, and we were listening to some music. A group of about eight young black men between the ages of ten and fifteen were walking down the sidewalk in front of the strip mall. Intuitively, I sensed they were going to start some trouble with us. I offered up a quick thanks for God's protection in our lives.

When the boys got close to our car, one of the youngest in the group started to step off the sidewalk toward me. The oldest-looking boy in the group grabbed his arm and said, "No, man. Don't." The boys walked a few more steps and turned around the corner of the strip mall onto a side street.

My wife saw the boys walk by, but she didn't notice anything else. I asked her if she thought we should offer to buy them a pizza. She smiled and said, "Yeah."

I walked around the corner, and the boys were about twenty yards away. The young one who was going to start trouble saw me and said, "Hey, guys. Look." Then he pulled a gun out of his pants and pointed it directly at my face. The oldest-looking boy once again intervened and grabbed the gun from him. Then he asked me, "What do you want?"

A little shaken, I said, "I want to buy you guys a pizza, if you want one."

He said, "Really?"

"Yeah."

"Why would you want to buy us a pizza?" he asked.

I responded, "Just to do something nice for you. Do you want one?"

He said, "Yeah," and they all walked toward me. I asked what kind they wanted and went inside to order it.

While I was inside, the boys asked my wife if I was a cop and was I trying to bust them. She said no. They also asked her why I wanted to buy them a pizza. She explained that we like to be generous.

I came out and waited with the boys while the pizza cooked. I talked with them about their hopes and dreams, though they didn't seem to have any. They were quiet and reserved, and very thankful when the pizza was ready. I talked to them a few minutes about having faith for good things to happen to them, and then we said good-bye.

Being generous is a witness to others of

kindness and love. It benefits the giver as much as, maybe even more than, the receiver.

Millionaires believe they must be generous.

3

Millionaires have multiple sources of income.

Let's compare dollars to fish. Would a fisherman catch more fish if he had two lines in the water? Of course. There is a greater possibility that he would. What if he had five lines in the water? It's easy to see that the more lines he has in the water, the more fish he has the possibility of catching.

Money is like that. The more sources of income you can develop, the more likely it is you

will become a million-
aire. For every million-
aire who has achieved
her wealth doing only
one thing, there are a
dozen others who be-

> The more sources of income you can develop, the more likely it is you will become a millionaire.

came financially free by combining several forms
of income.

Passive Income

The trick to developing multiple sources of
income is to focus on making them passive
income. By *passive* I don't mean you won't have
to work. I mean they require little maintenance
or management from you personally.

Many millionaires have the ability to put
together teams that can run their businesses
better than they could do it on their own. People
in the middle class have a difficult time with the
idea of multiple sources of income because they
think they must do everything themselves.

The belief that you must do everything your-self puts extreme limits on your financial poten-tial. Having a belief that no one can do it as well as you is arrogance. The world is full of talented people.

Millionaires have a different belief. They be-lieve they can find someone who can do it not only as well as they can, but even better! What a contrast!

Build a Team

Millionaires have also developed the special skill of getting people to work well together, which pays handsomely. It is a skill, however, that takes time to develop. It is the ability to get peo-ple to embrace one another's differences and to assign the right person to the right position.

Many companies struggle simply because they have the wrong people in the wrong posi-tions. Getting people to work well together means you must develop an atmosphere of trust. Millionaires build teams of people who complement one another, not compete with one another. When you have team members who compete with one another, it is difficult to get them to trust one another. There is no limit to what can be accomplished if it doesn't matter who gets the credit. People who trust one another can accomplish far more than any one person could on his or her own.

In order to develop trust within your team you must establish a code of honor. A code of honor is a set of simple rules that everyone is committed to playing by. If you are in the early stages of putting together a team, it is beneficial to let the team develop the code. If you bring in a team member after the code has been developed, then the new member must agree to play by the rules or he or she doesn't get the job. If someone does anything against the code, then it is the team's responsibility to call him or her on it.

The power of a code of honor is only effective if people are questioned when they violate it. What good is a code if you are not going to enforce it? When building a team, everyone must be willing to accept correction from other team members. If team members get angry or offended when corrected, then they must change their attitude or leave the team.

Anger has no place in a winning team. Anger is a sign of arrogance. There is power in humility, and teams that develop a humble attitude will accomplish great things. Millionaires bring a spirit of humility to their teams because they are humble themselves. To be humble is to be teachable.

Millionaires are always open to learning better ways to run their businesses. Millionaires understand that sales equals income but massive income equals having a team built on the foundation of trust.

Practice Intentional Congruence

Let's look at a term I learned from my mentor Nido Qubein—*intentional congruence*. It is the essence of how to create successful multiple sources of income. *Intentional* means: doing something on purpose. A planned event. A thought-out action. *Congruence* means: connected. Alignment. Agreement. Things work well together.

Intentional congruence is practiced by the very wealthy. It is methodical planning. The power of intentional congruence is getting each source of passive income to support the others.

When you first start a new source of income, you must focus on it. Focus is power, and all millionaires possess this power. There are two ways you need to focus in order to put intentional congruence to work in your life. You must focus like a laser on specific parts of the big picture of your life. And you must learn to focus like a spotlight on the entire big picture.

Anyone can focus on *one* thing. It requires a powerful person to focus on the big picture and get all the parts working together. Having multiple sources of passive income that have nothing to do with one another is still better than having only one or two sources. However, learning to build passive income streams that feed one another will make you much more money over time.

Back to the fisherman. It is easy to see how four or five lines in the water will catch more fish than just one. What happens with intentional congruence is even better than multiple lines in the water. Intentional congruence is having a net. I ask you, who is going to catch more fish, the fisherman who uses individual lines or the one who uses a net? Intentional congruence connects each business you are involved in and assists each one in making more money.

The concept of intentional congruence is first and foremost intentional. It doesn't happen by accident. If you currently have one source of income and want to start another source, then make sure the new source of income supports the first, and make sure the first source can support the new one. Do they help promote each other? Can your primary source of income do business with your secondary or third? Do they lend credibility to each other? Can the customers from your primary source also become customers of your new endeavor?

Intentional congruence is relatively new for most people and requires serious thought. It takes time to develop businesses that are congruent with each other. Over time, intentional congruence will work miracles in your financial life.

The middle class believes that if you attempt to build multiple sources of income, you will spread yourself too thin. Once again, that's because they think they must do it themselves. If a middle-class person has more than one source of income, it is usually a second job where he or she does the work. And you can bet it is probably not intentionally connected to the first job.

If you focus on PASSIVE sources of income, build a TEAM, and practice INTENTIONAL CONGRUENCE, it is impossible to spread yourself too thin. You must be careful, however, not to let the middle-class mind-set keep you from taking action and trying new things. Passive income, teams, and intentional congruence are a three-strand cord that is not easily broken. They build a strong financial life.

Millionaires have multiple
sources of income.

2

Millionaires focus on increasing their net worth.

Most everyone has heard the saying "Work smarter, not harder." Focusing on your net worth is working smart. Working for a paycheck is working hard.

Millionaires attain financial freedom because they work hard in the beginning to build their net worth. Once their net worth is built to a certain level, they are free to do what they want, when they want.

The middle class is trapped in the rat race. The rat race is: get up, go to work, pay bills, get up, go to work, pay bills, get up, go to work, pay bills. . . . Millionaires get up, do what they love, spend time with their families, donate to causes they believe in, travel to exotic places, and continually look for investments to increase their net worth.

A Millionaire's Definition of Net Worth

The typical definition of *net worth* is assets minus liabilities. Most people think an asset is anything they own that has value. While this is the definition most people use, it is not the way millionaires think about assets; and, when it comes to money, it is wiser to think like a millionaire than like most people.

Millionaires look at assets as the things they own that have value *and* earn passive income for them. A middle-class person may have small assets that have some value, but these assets typically don't produce a passive income. So, please think about an asset as something of value that also produces a passive income for you.

Your liabilities are the things you owe money for, like mortgages, car payments, credit card debts, and school and personal loans. Subtract the amount of money you owe from the things you own that have value and produce passive income. This figure is your true net worth. A net worth that doesn't produce a passive income is worthless as far as millionaires are concerned. Millionaires focus on increasing their net worth, which simultaneously increases their passive income.

Millionaires make their money work hard for them. The middle class works hard for its money.

There are two reasons why working for a paycheck alone is risky

> Millionaires make their money work hard for them. The middle class works hard for its money.

and not very smart. One, as your paycheck gets bigger, so do your taxes. Two, as your paycheck gets bigger, so does your dependence on someone else.

Millionaires are in control of their financial lives. Middle-class people place control of their financial lives in the hands of someone else. If you work for a paycheck, the government is in control of how much you pay in taxes. Millionaires control how much they pay in taxes and when they pay taxes. Your employer is in control of whether you will have a job next month. The middle class never knows when a company may downsize. Because middle-class people depend on someone else for their finances, they are always at risk of losing their income.

A couple of my friends are airline pilots. They were fortunate enough not to lose their jobs after 9/11, but they did lose about 30 percent of their income overnight. What would happen if you lost 30 percent of your income tomorrow? Millionaires know they will have income next month and next year.

Turn Your Paycheck Into Passive Income

Working for a paycheck is not wrong or bad, it's just hard work for most people—and it is risky. Many people who are millionaires today once worked for a paycheck. How did they become financially free? By using their paychecks to buy assets. Most millionaires had a season in their lives when they worked a lot. They worked hard to buy assets.

Buying assets that produce passive income is not easy at first. It requires new knowledge, which is gained by many hours of personal study. Millionaires not only work hard, they also study hard to learn how to acquire income-producing assets. Increasing your net worth with assets that produce passive income is a skill

Patience, knowledge, and wisdom are required to increase your net worth.

and skills require time to develop. Patience, knowledge, and wisdom are required to increase your net worth.

Be patient with yourself, gain knowledge about assets, and then use wisdom.

Wisdom is the application of knowledge. Some middle-class people have knowledge about passive income and increasing their net worth, but they haven't yet applied it.

Millionaires apply the knowledge they gain. They also continually increase their knowledge. Millionaires have knowledge of and invest in some things that the middle class doesn't even know exist.

It is beyond the scope of this book to talk about all of the many assets millionaires invest in for passive income, so I will mention a few of the most well known that most millionaires started with when they were still in the middle class.

Start a Small Business

In my opinion, everyone should have a small business. I am not saying to quit your job and start a business. I am suggesting you start a part-time business while working at your current job.

One way of doing this is to join a network marketing company. Direct sales or network marketing companies are a great way to start your own business. They are very low risk with the possibility of a very high reward. They have proven systems in place that work and offer continual support to help you. They are a great way to be in business for yourself but not by yourself. I have three recommendations if you are considering joining a network marketing company:

1. Make sure you sincerely believe in the products or service.
2. Make sure you feel at peace with the people you meet.

3. Make sure the company is involved in some kind of charitable work.

If these three requirements are met, then I believe you can create a very successful part-time business. When joining a network marketing company or starting any small business, set the goal to earn more from your part-time business than you do from your full-time job. After you achieve that, you will have the freedom to work because you *want* to instead of because you *have* to. Wouldn't that be nice?

When you start your own business, make sure you keep your cost of living the same and save the money you make from your new business until you are ready to invest in an asset. It is the most common thing in the world to spend more money when you start making more money. I did it for years. Every time I earned more money, I would buy a nicer car, move into a larger house, and take a vacation to Hawaii. I can say from experience that it is not wise to increase your cost of living until you can pay for it with the passive income from your assets.

Millionaires have uncommon wisdom; they do not increase their spending when their income increases, they increase their investing. The middle class spends its income on liabilities; millionaires invest their income in assets. Investing in assets that produce passive income is the essence of wealth building.

> Millionaires do not increase their spending when their income increases, they increase their investing.

Perhaps the greatest advantage of owning your own business is the tax advantage. Business owners can write off several things that you can't as an employee. I am not a tax attorney or tax strategist, so I will not offer advice here, but you absolutely must learn about the tax advantages you are entitled to as a business owner.

Business owners are able to spend the money

they make before they get taxed. When you work for a paycheck, you must pay taxes first; then you get to spend the little bit that's left over. Millionaires make money, spend it, and then pay taxes. The middle class makes money, pays taxes, and then spends what's left.

Would you like to pay less in taxes? Start a small business. A small business can give you great tax advantages and it can become an asset if you set it up so that it doesn't demand much of your personal time. Remember, a million-aire's definition of an asset is something of value that produces passive income. Also remember, *passive* income doesn't mean you don't do any-thing; it means you only have to do a bit of management.

Invest in Real Estate

In my opinion, real estate is the best and safest asset to invest in. Almost all millionaires receive passive income from real estate. Few middle-class people have passive income from real estate. Bookstores are full of books on how to invest in real estate, so I will not discuss it here. I suggest you read books on real estate until you become knowledgeable enough to take action and start investing in it. I can honestly say my financial life totally changed when I started investing in real estate.

What About Stocks?

Most millionaires invest in the stock market. I say "most" because I know some millionaires who only invest in real estate. On the other hand, I also know some who only invest in stocks. Stocks can be a great form of passive income. They can also be risky if you are not knowledgeable about them.

Small businesses, real estate, and stocks all have certain risks. However, the risks are greatly

> Remember, if you take risk out of life, you take opportunity out of life.

reduced as you increase your knowledge. Remember, if you take risk out of life, you take opportunity out of life. Risk is opportunity.

Net Worth Is Not a Nest Egg

The middle class thinks financial security is having a nest egg. Millionaires don't think like that. Millionaires don't have nest eggs; they have geese that lay golden eggs on a consistent basis. Millionaires' net worths are their geese. The passive incomes they receive from their net worth are the golden eggs.

The problem with the nest egg mentality is that you can get hungry and end up scrambling and eating it. The middle class loves scrambled eggs! Millionaires check on their geese often to make sure they are healthy. Most of the middle class never even looks at its net worth.

Focus on increasing your net worth with assets that produce passive income and the day will come when you are totally financially free.

Millionaires focus on increasing their net worth.

1

Millionaires ask themselves empowering questions.

On the surface this distinction may seem unimportant; I assure you it is a profound principle. When you develop the habit of asking yourself empowering questions, your life will take on new meaning and success is inevitable.

This distinction reflects a universal principle that is summed up in the ancient scripture "Ask and you will receive."

You will receive answers for whatever

questions you ask, so you better ask empowering questions. The bigger your questions the bet-

ter. Learn to ask
yourself questions that
stretch you beyond
your current levels of
experience. Questions
hold the answers that
you need to succeed.

> Learn to ask yourself
> questions that stretch
> you beyond your
> current levels of
> experience.

Examples of Empowering Questions

Which question is more empowering, "How can
I double my income this year?" or "How can I
get enough money to pay the bills this month?"

Do you see the difference? It takes the same
amount of mental energy to think about answer-
ing the big question as it does the small question.
Think about questions that expand your mind,
because you will receive answers for any questions you ask.

Let's look at a few more examples. "How

can I make $1 million a year doing what I love?"
or "How can I get my boss to give me a raise?"

"What is life trying to teach me right now?"
or "Why do bad things always happen to me?"

"How can I develop a deeper relationship
with my spouse?" or "Why is it so hard to get
along with my spouse?"

"What can I do to show my kids I love them
today?" or "Why don't my kids appreciate me?"

"What would I enjoy doing to stay strong
and healthy?" or "Why is it so hard to lose
weight?"

"Who can teach me to earn a minimum of 25
percent return on my investments?" or "Why is
it so hard to save money?"

"How can I increase my peace of mind?" or
"Why am I always stressed?"

Questions Control the Way You Feel

Empowering questions ask what you *can* do and
disempowering questions ask what you *can't* do.

Disempowering questions also ask why things are hard.

Empowering questions make you feel good. Disempowering questions make you feel bad. You can control the way you feel by asking yourself empowering questions.

Millionaires are masters at managing their emotions. They are masters at it because they habitually ask themselves empowering questions.

When empowering questions become a part of your habitual way of thinking, you become a powerful and peaceful person. Empowering questions cause you to reach for your full potential. The questions you ask yourself determine the results you get in your life. If you feel like you are not living up to your potential, one reason is because you are asking yourself disempowering questions. As simple as that may sound, it is the truth.

> The questions you ask yourself determine the results you get in your life.

Millionaires ask questions that make them rich. Middle-class people ask questions that keep them poor.

Conditioning Your Mind

Most middle-class people are unaware or unconscious of the questions they ask themselves on a regular basis. I observe this all the time in my conversations with middle-class people. It amazes me how I can control conversations by asking questions and how middle-class people move their trains of thought to wherever I want to lead them. I used to hate being around people who talked about things and other people—until I discovered the power of questions. Now I don't mind because I can easily change the conversation to something more positive simply by asking questions.

Millionaires are aware of the questions they ask themselves. They are conscious of their thoughts. They continually work on conditioning their minds to lead them to more success. This universal principle is also summed up in ancient scripture: "As a man thinks, so is he."

The problem with middle-class people is they don't think for themselves. They believe they do, but in actuality other people control their thinking.

Proof of this can be found in Distinction 9, "Millionaires talk about ideas. The middle class talks about things and other people." The reason middle-class people always talk about things and other people is because their minds are simply reacting to what other people say and do.

Millionaires are more creative than reactive. By asking themselves empowering questions, they control their minds.

Asking yourself empowering questions is one of the best ways to condition your mind to create success.

> Asking yourself empowering questions is one of the best ways to condition your mind to create success.

We are all conditioned to think the way we do. Millionaires consciously condition their minds. By controlling the questions you ask your-

> You gain control of your life by controlling your internal dialogue.

self, you will learn to think for yourself. You gain control of your life by controlling your in-

ternal dialogue. You must become aware of the questions you ask yourself if you want to become more successful.

Nine Empowering
Questions

I want to ask you nine empowering questions that everyone must answer in order to achieve true success and happiness. These questions deal with who you want to be, what you want to do, and what you want to have. If you take the time to answer these questions honestly, you will find yourself on the path to success.

What kind of person do I want to be?

Why do I want to be that kind of person?

How can I become that kind of person?

What do I want to do?

Why do I want to do it?

How can I do it?

What do I want to have?

Why do I want to have it?

How can I create it?

Your answers to these questions must be clear. By *clear*, I mean *specific*. The more specific your answers to these questions the better.

Clarity is power. Millionaires know what they want. More important, they know why they want it. And because they have decided *what*

> Clarity is power.
> Millionaires know what they want.

and *why,* they are able to find *how.* The middle class doesn't know how to become millionaires because it doesn't have an exciting *what* or an empowering *why.*

When you answer the *why* questions, you may discover that you are becoming who someone else wanted you to become. Or that you are doing things other people wanted you to do—but you don't really want to. Or that you desire things because others told you to. Trying to live up to the expectations of others is a trap.

Discover who you really want to be, what you really want to do, and what you really want to have.

Make sure you keep these questions in the "be, do, have" order. The type of person you want to be should determine what you want to do and have.

Many people in the middle class have this

backward. They think what they have determines what they do; and what they do
determines what kind of person they are. Looking at life like this is a sure way to experience
confusion. Who I am determines what I do and
what I have.

Instead of asking "What's the meaning of my
life?" ask, "What would make my life meaningful?" That is a more empowering question. Your
honest answer to the second question will reveal
the answer to the first question.

The meaning of our lives is not to HAVE success but to BE successful.

Asking yourself who you are becoming is,
perhaps, the most empowering question. For
centuries people have asked themselves the
question "Who am I?" I suggest you ask yourself,
"Who am I becoming?" If you don't like your
answer to that question, then ask, "Who do I
want to become?" and do whatever it takes to

become that kind of person. Being a millionaire is about being, doing, and then having.

Millionaires ask themselves empowering questions.

Now What?

1. Read this little book again and again. I recommend reading it once a month until you feel the ten habits have become a part of who you are. Repetition is the primary way we train our minds to think differently. When we think differently, we act differently and achieve different results.

2. Share copies of this book with the appropriate people in your life so you can discuss the habits and learn from one another's experiences and perspectives.

3. Go to www.keithcameronsmith.com and register for the Wise Distinctions e-mail to have

continued support in developing your mind-set for success and fulfillment. You can also join me for teleseminars and get information about a Wisdom Creates Freedom workshop or seminar.

KEITH CAMERON SMITH is an entrepreneur and inspirational speaker who teaches his financial success principles to individuals and companies around the country. The author of *The Spiritual Millionaire,* Smith lives in Ormond Beach, Florida, with his wife and two young children. Visit his website, keithcameronsmith.com.

ABOUT THE TYPE

This book was set in Sabon, a typeface designed by the well-known German typographer Jan Tschichold (1902–74). Sabon's design is based upon the original letter forms of Claude Garamond and was created specifically to be used for three sources: foundry type for hand composition, Linotype, and Monotype. Tschichold named his typeface for the famous Frankfurt typefounder Jacques Sabon, who died in 1580.